Pugs

by Nico Barnes

Visit us at www.abdopublishing.com

Published by Abdo Kids, a division of ABDO, P.O. Box 398166, Minneapolis, Minnesota 55439.

Printed in the United States of America, North Mankato, Minnesota.

032014
092014

 PRINTED ON RECYCLED PAPER

Photo Credits: Glow Images, iStock, Shutterstock, Thinkstock
Production Contributors: Teddy Borth, Jennie Forsberg, Grace Hansen
Design Contributors: Dorothy Toth, Renée LaViolette, Laura Rask

Library of Congress Control Number: 2013952557
Cataloging-in-Publication Data
Barnes, Nico.
 Pugs / Nico Barnes.
   p. cm. -- (Dogs)
ISBN 978-1-62970-034-2 (lib. bdg.)
Includes bibliographical references and index.
1. Pugs--Juvenile literature.   I. Title.
636.76--dc23
                    2013952557

Table of Contents

Pugs

Pugs are fun and loving.

They make great pets!

5

Pugs are toy dogs. That means they are small. Even though pugs are small, they are strong.

6

Pugs come in many colors.

Usually, they are tan or black.

9

A pug's face is short and flat.

It has thick **wrinkles**.

Pugs have black **muzzles**.

Their coats are short and **shiny**.

Pugs are known for their curly tails! They are also known for their large eyes.

14

Exercise

Pugs do not need a lot of exercise. Their flat faces make it hard for them to breathe. But they do **enjoy** walks with their families.

16

Personality

Pugs love to sleep. Some will sleep 14 hours a day!

When pugs are awake,

they are silly and playful.

20

More Facts

- Pugs were originally bred in China.

- Pugs are one of the oldest dog breeds.

- Pugs are one of the few dogs that don't mind wearing a funny costume!

Glossary

enjoy – to find happiness in.

muzzle – an animal's nose and jaw.

shiny – bright and glossy.

wrinkle – a line or fold in the skin.

Index

abdokids.com

Use this code to log on to abdokids.com and access crafts, games, videos and more!

Abdo Kids Code:
DPK0342